Read-About® Geography

Michigan

By Jan Mader

Consultant
Jeanne Clidas, Ph.D.
National Reading Consultant
and
Professor of Reading, SUNY Brockport

D0003462

 Children's Press~
A Division of Scholastic Inc.
New York   Toronto   London   Auckland   Sydney
Mexico City   New Delhi   Hong Kong
Danbury, Connecticut

Designer: Herman Adler Design
Photo Researcher: Caroline Anderson
The photo on the cover shows Wagner Falls.

Library of Congress Cataloging-in-Publication Data

Mader, Jan.
　Michigan / by Jan Mader.
　　　p. cm. – (Rookie read-about geography)
Includes index.
Summary: A simple introduction to Michigan, focusing on its geographical
features and points of interest.
　ISBN 0-516-22736-X (lib. bdg.)　　　　　0-516-27781-2 (pbk.)
　1. Michigan–Juvenile literature. 2. Michigan–Geography–Juvenile
literature. [1. Michigan.] I. Title. II. Series.
　F566.3 .M23 2003
　917.74—dc21
　　　　　　　　　　　　　　　　　　　2002011561

1 2 3 4 5 6 7 8 9 10 R 12 11 10 09 08 07 06 05 04 03

Do you know which state
is shaped like a mitten?

It is Michigan!

Michigan has two parts called the Upper Peninsula and the Lower Peninsula.

A peninsula (puh-NIN-suh-luh) has water on three sides of the land. The Lower Peninsula is shaped like a mitten.

CANADA

WASHINGTON

OREGON

IDAHO

MONTANA

NORTH DAKOTA

SOUTH DAKOTA

WYOMING

NEVADA

UTAH

CALIFORNIA

ARIZONA

COLORADO

NEW MEXICO

MINNESOTA

WISCONSIN

MICHIGAN

IOWA

NEBRASKA

KANSAS

OKLAHOMA

TEXAS

MISSOURI

ARKANSAS

LOUISIANA

ILLINOIS

INDIANA

OHIO

KENTUCKY

TENNESSEE

MISSISSIPPI

ALABAMA

NEW HAMPSHIRE

VERMONT

MAINE

NEW YORK

MASSACHUSETTS

RHODE ISLAND

CONNECTICUT

PENNSYLVANIA

NEW JERSEY

WEST VIRGINIA

DELAWARE

MARYLAND

Washington, D.C.

VIRGINIA

NORTH CAROLINA

SOUTH CAROLINA

GEORGIA

FLORIDA

North

West

East

South

ALASKA

CANADA

MEXICO

HAWAII

5

You must cross the Mackinac Bridge to get from one peninsula to the other.

Michigan is known as
the Great Lakes State.
It touches Lake Superior,
Lake Huron, Lake Erie
(EE-ree), and Lake Michigan.

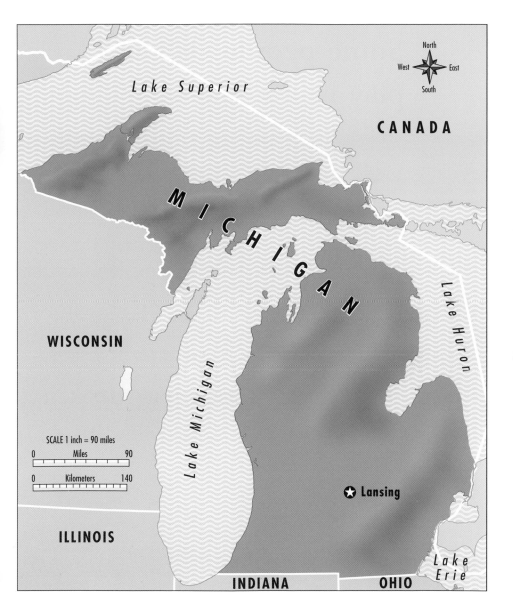

Lake Superior

CANADA

MICHIGAN

WISCONSIN

Lake Michigan

Lake Huron

SCALE 1 inch = 90 miles

| 0 | Miles | 90 |

| 0 | Kilometers | 140 |

★ Lansing

ILLINOIS

INDIANA

OHIO

Lake Erie

North
West East
South

Some people fish and play in the lakes.

There are big ships called
freighters (FRAY-turz)
on the lakes. They move
steel, cars, and many other
things to places far away.

This is one of the ways
people use the lakes to
help them work.

People in Michigan do many kinds of work. They work in offices, stores, schools, and banks. Some people work on farms.

Some people in Michigan may
work in factories making cars.

Detroit is a big city in Michigan. It is known as "Motor City" because so many cars are made there.

You can see how cars
used to look in Dearborn,
Michigan. You will find
the Henry Ford Museum
(myoo-ZEE-um) there.
A museum is a place
people go to look at
interesting things.

Henry Ford invented
one of the first cars.

Half of Michigan is covered with forests. Many animals live in the forests.

The state bird of Michigan is the robin.

Have you ever heard Michigan called the "Wolverine (WUL-vuh-reen) State"?

Trappers used to catch these small animals and trade their furs. There are no wolverines in Michigan now. Their relatives are the muskrats, beavers, badgers, and weasels. These animals still live there.

The University of Michigan is in Ann Arbor. The football team is called the Michigan Wolverines.

Winters in the Upper
Peninsula can be very cold.

Summers in the Lower Peninsula are warm. The land in the Lower Peninsula is good for growing fruit.

The children in Michigan love the snow. Sledding and skiing are great fun!

What would you like to see and do in Michigan?

Words You Know

beaver

factory

freighter

Henry Ford Museum

lake

Mackinac Bridge

robin

Index

About the Author

Jan Mader has been writing for children for 15 years. Her natural curiosity and joy of life characterize her work in more than 24 published easy-reader stories.

Photo Credits

Photographs © 2003: AP/Wide World Photos/Doug Bauman/The Oakland Press: 14; Dembinsky Photo Assoc.: 26 (Claudia Adams), 23, 30 top left (Dominique Braud), 29 (Gary Bublitz), cover (Barbara Gerlach), 24 (Stephen Graham), 16 (Doug Locke), 21, 31 bottom right (Gary Meszaros), 7, 31 bottom left (Skip Moody), 17; Folio, Inc./David R. Frazier: 27; Getty Images/Brent Smith/Reuters: 25; Peter Arnold Inc.: 20 (Ed Reschke), 10 (Carl R. Sams II); PhotoEdit/Barbara Stizer: 3; Stone/Getty Images/Vito Palmisano: 11, 31 top right; Superstock, Inc.: 15, 19, 30 top right, 31 top left; The Image Works: 12, 30 bottom (Townsend P. Dickinson), 19 inset (Topham).

Maps by Bob Italiano